AT HIS FEET IN CONFESSION

Discovering a New Way of Loving God

AT HIS FEET IN CONFESSION

Discovering a New Way of Loving God

By

Marc Bastawrous

ST SHENOUDA PRESS
SYDNEY, AUSTRALIA
2022

At His Feet In Confession:
Discovering a New Way of Loving God

COPYRIGHT © 2022
St Shenouda Press

All rights reserved. Except for brief quotations in critical publications or reviews, no part of this book may be reproduced in any manner without prior written permission from the publisher.

ST SHENOUDA PRESS
8419 Putty Rd,
Putty, NSW, 2330
Sydney, Australia

www.stshenoudapress.com

ISBN 13: 978-0-6455543-5-9

All scripture quotations, unless otherwise indicated, are taken from the New King James Version®. Copyright © 1982 by Thomas Nelson, Inc. Used by permission. All rights reserved.

About the Author:
Marc Bastawrous attends St Mark's Coptic Orthodox Church, Sydney where he is heavily involved in youth ministry and sunday school. He has completed studying medicine at Bond University and currently works as a Doctor in Australia. He is a regular blogger on the Upper Room media app. He writes about many topics relating to the Orthodox faith.

Cover Design:
Dionysia Tanios
@dionysiandesigns

Contents

Section 1

Introduction	7
Questions & Answers	13
Conclusion	65
Fianl Words	69

Section 2

Introduction	73
The Gospel According to St Luke	75
For She Loved Much By: Saint Ephraim the Syrian	77
Recommended Readings	87

Section 1

Questions & Answers

Introduction

"If ever there was a doubt that Christ lives and breathes in people, you need only look to my husband for proof otherwise," the grieving widow began her eulogy, "he was a good man."

It was a pleasant wake. Close family and friends gathered at the poor widows' home to pay their respects and offer condolences. It seemed though, that she was not all that interested in receiving condolences. She was more concerned with sharing stories of her late husband. In fact, to many of the attendees she appeared almost joyful. The sight of a widow, who had just lost her husband and had no children to care for her, smiling, was odd to say the least. A friend could no longer contain herself. Following the wake, she approached the widow and asked her, "Woman, why are you not grieving?"

She responded with a story.
"For forty years, my husband and I have been married but it wasn't always so lovely. When we were much younger, I fell out of love with him. The relationship began to grow stale. I felt a numbness towards him as we drifted apart day by day until, I ended up in the arms of another. I

carried the guilt of my betrayal about with me like chains around my neck until I confronted him and confessed my adultery. His response frightened me. He said not a single word. In fact, his expression barely changed. He simply looked me in the eyes and then looked away, all the while maintaining a deafening silence."

"In the days that followed, he began to do something out of character. He would return late from work, as he often did, and would make his way to the wardrobe in our room where we used to pray together, without ever looking at me once. Some nights he would spend mere minutes in there, other nights he would remain in the wardrobe for hours, but one thing never changed. No matter how long he spent in the wardrobe, he never spoke a single word. He remained silent."

"Finally, after perhaps two months of following this strict canon, he emerged from the wardrobe and left the room altogether. He made his way downstairs, went to our kitchen to fetch a large basin and filled it with water. He returned to our room, lifted me off our bed, placed my feet in the basin of water and with tears falling down his cheeks, he began to wash my feet. My heart raced as he began speaking to me for the first time. It was as though I had forgotten the sound of his voice. He began by saying, 'for so long I have forgotten you and I neglected my responsibilities towards you. Whenever I noticed you were sad or angry, I forgot to console you and give you the comfort you needed. Whenever I returned home and found you cleaning or preparing dinner for us, I forgot to show you my gratitude and I never gave you the appreciation you craved. Whenever you returned home after a long day of work, tired and feeling broken, I never prepared food for you to eat or a hot bath for you to relax. I never

Introduction

washed your feet. For so long, I overlooked your need for tenderness and love. Yes, you betrayed me, but it was all my own doing. I am the one who pushed you away.'"

The widow began to sob as she continued her tale. "What he did next completely broke me. He looked up into my eyes-the first time he looked at me in so long-and he asked, 'could you ever forgive me?' I wept uncontrollably in his arms, begging him to put the blame on me and forgive me, but he insisted I forgive him. We held each other the entire night. My heart exploded with tremendous love for him, just as I felt his for me. It was as though our hearts had awoken to each other. His life was an echo of the life of Christ Himself, and for this reason, I will never grieve his memory."

Her friend was brought to tears and curiously she enquired, "Surely, he would not want you to grieve. But why, dear sister, do you smile?"

"That is simple," the widow replied, "because the Lord has been waiting all this time to wash his feet."

This story is a picture of true repentance. The question though is, who is 'the repented' in the story? Some might say that it was the wife, who took upon the humiliation of confessing her sin to her husband, begging him for forgiveness. Others might say that it was the husband, who found fault in himself and actively showed his remorse by washing her feet and also requesting her absolution. In actual fact, both the husband and his wife took on the role of the repented in this tale.

The confession of the wife is frequently how we view the notion of repentance. But let us look to the husband in this story as an example of profound metanoia[1]. Repentance,

---
1   Def: metanoia - a change of mind, as it appears to one who repents, of a

as we will come to read, is as simple as a turning of the mind and heart towards God. In turning towards God – by spending time in complete isolation with Him within the confines of his wardrobe – the husband uncovered the extreme measures of God's love, which overflowed into overwhelming forgiveness. It is unfathomable to believe that the man could have found it in his heart to show forgiveness outside of this alone time with God. This is real repentance. In turning towards God, we are given the ability to forgive the unforgivable, to love the unlovable and to show mercy where only justice is due.

In his book 'Soul Mending', John Chryssavgis, an Archdeacon of the Greek Orthodox Archdiocese of America and theologian, defines repentance as the following:

"Repentance is simply a new way of loving God every day."[2]

It is within the territories of this definition, that we most clearly see the husband in his repented state. We know through passages of scripture that we love God by loving others. In finding a way to love his adulterous wife, the husband discovered a new way of loving God. No doubt this process broke him. For sure it revealed to him the dark pits of his identity. However, while the journey may have been tiresome and trying, the destination was beautiful.

By learning this, we come to understand the profound words of the Greek poet, Nikiforus Vrettakos, as he writes with striking imagery in his stunning poem, "The First Thing of Creation":

I don't know how

But suddenly there is no darkness left at all

---

purpose he has formed or of something he has done
2   Chryssavgis J, Soul Mending: *The Art of Spiritual Direction*, Holy Cross Orthodox Press, 2000, ix

Questions and Answers

The sun has poured itself inside me

From a thousand wounds[3]

It would be improper though to ignore the husbands final act within the tale. Almost as if he had emerged from the tomb, the husband walked out of the wardrobe and washed the feet of his wife. Thus, proving to the reader the single and most crucial thing to note about repentance – it is active. It is not enough to rise after weeping over my sins and crying out for forgiveness, I must now live different. If I am to find a new way to love, it will not be in the prayers I speak or the confessions I utter, but in the way I live. True repentance is to awaken from my sleep and put on the life of Christ who now, just like in the life of the husband from the tale, lives and breathes within me.

---

[3] Nikiforus Vrettakos, *Selected Poems*

Q1   Repentance: What is it?

How else could we grasp the journey of repentance without first being enlightened to what it entails? Inevitably, when we think about the concept of repentance, we believe that it is a state of feeling sorry for ourselves or experiencing a tremendous sense of guilt over our sins. Whilst these emotions may at times be present during repentance, they do not define the state of being repentant.

Pope Shenouda III simply explains that, "true repentance is a human longing for the origin from which we were taken. It is the desire of a heart that strayed from God, and finally felt it could go no further away."[4] St Macarius the Great also views repentance as the journey back into the company of God where we belong, saying: "Just as God has created heaven and earth for man to inhabit, so He has created the body and the soul of a man to be His abode, that is why the Apostle says, 'His house we are' (Heb 3:6)."[5]

The word itself is indicative of this desire to turn back to its original source. 'Repentance' derives from the Greek word metanoia meaning "a change of heart or mind" - 'meta' meaning "to change" or "transform" and 'nous' meaning "mind" or "heart". This is where the concept of 'metanya' in the Orthodox church arises from. Thus, whenever we offer prostrations in prayer, our minds ought to contemplate on and desire this change of heart. Imagine a sprinter running very fast in one direction, when suddenly, they are picked up from the ground with their legs still kicking violently. That sprinter is then turned around and placed back on the ground, effectively running at the same speed but in the

---

[4]   Pope Shenouda III, *The Life of Repentance and Purity*, SVS Press, 2016, 17
[5]   St Macarius the Great, *Spiritual Discourses – Epistles and Speeches*, 4th Edition, Holy Trinity, St Sergius Lavra, 1904

opposite direction. That is the image of true repentance. The term is used to suggest a state of spiritual conversion or reform and is used consistently throughout the New Testament. In fact, its first use in the New Testament comes directly from the mouth of Christ in Mark chapter 1, where He implores the multitudes to, "Repent and believe in the Gospel."[6] The idea of repentance being associated with 'sorrow' is also present in the New Testament and is derived from the Greek word metamelomai. However, this word is used ten times less than the aforementioned metanoia and is most famously used in the case of Judas when Mark writes, "seeing that He had been condemned, was remorseful (metamelomai) and brought back the thirty pieces of silver to the chief priests and elders."[7]

Hence, this idea of changing one's mind formed the foundation of the preaching of the early church as the disciples pleaded with everyone to essentially change their way of thinking and "return" to the Lord, as we so often see in the case of the Old Testament prophets.

One such example in the Old Testament is found in the book of Jeremiah the Prophet, when he quotes God and proclaims:

"'Return, backsliding Israel,' says the Lord; 'I will not cause My anger to fall on you. For I am merciful,' says the Lord"[8]

The Lord is making it very clear that He does not wish to pour out anger on those who return to Him but rather, mercy. This sentiment is repeated two more times within the same chapter as He goes on to say:

"Return, O backsliding children," says the Lord; "for I am

---

6   Mark 1:15 NKJV
7   Matt 27:3 NKJV
8   Jeremiah 3:12 NKJV

married to you."[9]
And then again:
"Return, you backsliding children, And I will heal your backslidings." [10]

In this chapter of Jeremiah alone, God wants to highlight to the people the true consequences of their repentance and His role in it. He will show mercy, He will renew the marriage covenant between them, and He will ultimately provide healing.

Picture a boy who runs away from home. Should the boy return many days later, wearing torn up clothes, bruised and battered from the long walk home, hungry and dehydrated; will the father of the boy rebuke his son for leaving? Or will he seek to heal him, feed him and quench his thirst? This is the picture of repentance, of 'metanoia.' Although we make ourselves far from Him, all that is required of us is to turn around, return to Him and He will 'heal' us as He promised the Israelites through the mouth of Jeremiah. Like this, repentance is not imagined as something that prompts feelings of shame or sorrow, but rather, a true sense of everlasting joy.

---

[9] Jeremiah 3:14 NKJV
[10] Jeremiah 3:22 NKJV

Q2 Why is it important to understand Repentance as a "change of heart" and not simply as sorrowful guilt?

While it is completely normal to feel a sense of grief in times of genuine repentance, there still remains a problem with repeatedly falling into this sensation. The problem is two-fold. The most obvious issue that exists is the capacity to fall into despair. Despair is feeling that, no matter how much I repent, I can never overcome my sin, or that my sin is far too grave to qualify for the forgiveness of God. It is a burden placed on us by the enemy who wishes only to break our spirit, a "war that tires many."[11] This diminishes the entire concept of returning to God. In the 4th century, St John Chrysostom warned his flock of such feelings:

"Repentance opens the heavens, takes us to Paradise, overcomes the devil. Have you sinned? Do not despair! If you sin every day, then offer repentance every day! When there are rotten parts in old houses, we replace the parts with new ones, and we do not stop caring for the houses. In the same way, you should reason for yourself: If today you have defiled yourself with sin, immediately cleanse yourself by returning to God."[12]

The second problem that exists, and the less subtle of the two, is that it makes my repentance completely dependent on me and my emotions. What if I don't feel sorry for my sin? What if I want to change but there isn't that feeling of guilt attached to my repentance? Does that make my repentance null? No, it shouldn't. Metanoia is beautiful in that it accepts that the heart cannot change of its own accord, but needs an external influence. It needs the influence of God.

---

11   Pope Shenouda III, *The Life of Repentance and Purity*, SVS Press, 2016, 31
12   Jim Forest, *Confession: Doorway to Forgiveness*, Orbis Books, 2002, 11

When God mapped out the plan to redeem humanity, He did so with a purpose in mind. He wanted to redeem us to Himself. Everything God did, since the beginning of time, was done with the purpose of inviting us to share in His love. To do so, He knew we would need to put away our old love for the things of the world and promised that, when He came to redeem us, He would resolve to give us a new heart and put a new spirit within us; He would take the heart of stone out of our flesh and give us a heart of flesh.[13] We needed Christ to do that. We couldn't do it on our own accord, no matter the amount of emotion or feeling I place into my repentance.

It does need to be said that there is value in feeling sorry over our sins. After all, sin is a separation from God and the love that He longs to share with us, what greater sorrow is there? However, dwelling on this after confession takes away from the joy that repentance should bring. I remember sitting with my confession father when he told me, "Repentance is a miracle. It is raising the dead back to life." When we approach confession, we share in the death of our Lord, and when we walk out, we are sharing in His resurrection. We have put off the old man and put on the resurrected Christ. Thus, it is important to share also in the joy of His resurrection. I have been granted a new heart and the old has well and truly passed away.

---

13   Ezekiel 36:26 NKJV

Q3 If I have been baptised by the "baptism that leads to life," then what need do I have for repentance?

"If baptism waters the seed of repentance which the word of God has planted within us, it remains for us to continually nurture this seeds growth."[14] Repentance is a renewal of the covenant made between us and God at the time of our baptism. It is, in essence, our baptism of choice – an active decision to turn towards and pursue a relationship with God. For many Christians born into the faith, they are baptised when they are still only very young. Their parents, in their wisdom, baptise them not long after their birth as a type of vaccination; in the hope that their children will be raised in the faith. Though this may be the case for many Christians, there comes a time when we must each make a deliberate decision to believe in and follow God. It is at this crossroads in life when repentance assumes the role of a second baptism. Not only is the second baptism a decision to turn to God, it is a turning to God for the forgiveness of our post-Baptismal sin. Though we may have been born into the faith from an early age, we each stray and require a kind of re-cleansing from our sin, "for all have sinned and fall short of the glory of God."[15] It is for this reason that Symeon the Theologian, in The Discourses, writes about our tears of repentance being our second baptism:

"Repentance gives rise to the tear from the depths of the soul; the tear cleanses the heart and wipes away great sins. When these have been blotted out through tears the soul finds itself in the comfort of the Spirit of God and is watered by tears of sweetest compunction."[16]

14　　John Chryssavgis, *Soul Mending: The Art of Spiritual Direction*, Holy Cross Orthodox Press, 2000, 5
15　　Romans 3:23 NKJV
16　　Symeon the Theologian, *The Discourses*, 160

It is, in essence, a baptism of tears. The power of this kind of baptism is made evident in the story of St Paësia that can be found (amongst many other beautiful stories of repentance) in Harlots of the Desert.[17] After being made an orphan from a very young age, Paësia turned her home into a hospice for the fathers of Scetis. Once her resources became exhausted, she fell heavily in want and turned to a life of prostitution to survive. St John the Short, hearing this, was troubled and went to see her to see if he could persuade her to turn away from harlotry. He stood at her door and implored her gatekeeper to allow him to see her, promising that he had something she wanted. Hearing that he was at the door, Paësia asked for him to be brought to her saying, 'these old men always search the Red Sea and find pearls.' As he was brought up to her room, she prepared herself and lay down on the bed. When John entered her room, he looked into her eyes and asked, 'what do you have against Jesus that you would act in this way?' She froze as she heard his words when, suddenly, John began weeping. She asked him, 'Father, why are you crying?' Looking again at her he replied, 'I see Satan playing with you my dear child, how could I not weep?' Hearing these troubling words she said to him, 'Father is it possible to repent?' The wise elder replied that it was possible, to which she beseeched him and said, 'Please take me wherever you wish.'

Abba John and Paësia made their way into the desert and when evening had come, John made a little pillow in the sand, marked it with a cross, said to her, 'sleep here,' and lay himself down to sleep. Upon waking in the middle of the night, John looked beside him to find that Paësia was no longer there and that there was a shining path reaching from the ground towards heaven. On this path he saw a legion of angels carrying her soul and on the ground in her place was a puddle of her tears. Seeing this scene unfold, he threw himself to the ground and while praying to God

---

17   Benedicta Ward SLG, *Harlots of the Desert*, 76-82

he heard the words:
'One single hour of repentance has brought her more than the penances of many who continue without showing such fervour in repentance.' [18]

Paësia, who from a very young age was recognised for her love and care for the monks, was baptised by her tears of repentance leading to eternal life after straying from the way she was brought up.

We are called to live this type of baptism daily, petitioning God to cleanse us from any temptations that may lead us far away from Him. It is for this reason that Chrysostom writes, "for this life, is in truth wholly devoted to repentance, penthos, and tears. Thus, it is necessary to repent, not merely for one or two days, but throughout one's life."[19] It is a continual, daily "renewal of baptism and is a contract with God for a fresh start in life."[20]

Q4 Sometimes the simple process of confessing seems so difficult. Is this normal?

There is no denying that the process of repentance and confession is challenging. It is a stripping away of all the things that, though we love, drive a wedge between us and our Father in Heaven. It is painful to admit that we have flaws and that we are weak, firstly before God but also before our father of confession. Yet, this is the path that leads directly to Christ.

"The very word confession makes us nervous, touching as it does all that is hidden in ourselves: lies told, injuries caused,

---
[18] John the Dwarf, *Sayings*, 40
[19] John Chrysostom, *De Compunctione I*, iPG 47:395 and I, ix: 408
[20] John Climacus, *The Ladder of Divine Ascent*, 121

Questions and Answers

things stolen, friends deceived, people betrayed, promises broken, faith denied––these plus all the smaller actions that reveal the beginnings of sins. Confession is painful, yet a Christian life without confession is impossible."[21]

No doubt this is why Malachi refers to the Lord as "a refiner and a purifier of silver,"[22] burning away all our impurities and defects until we are made perfect in His eyes. In fact, there is a beautiful story surrounding the message of this verse from the book of Malachi that a friend once shared with me.

There was a group of women attending a weekly Bible study. As they were studying, the third chapter of Malachi, they came across this verse which reads, "He will sit as a refiner and purifier of silver." This verse puzzled them, and they speculated what this statement meant about the character of God.

One of the women offered to find out about the process of refining silver and get back to the group at their next Bible study. That week the woman called up a silversmith and made an appointment to watch him at work. She didn't mention anything about the reason for her interest in silver beyond her curiosity about the process of refining silver. As she watched the silversmith, he held a piece of silver over the fire and let it heat up. He explained that, in refining silver, one needed to hold the silver in the middle of the fire where the flames were hottest so as to burn away all the impurities.

The woman thought about God holding us in such a hot spot - then she thought again about the verse, that He sits as a refiner and purifier of silver. She asked the silversmith

---

21   Jim Forest, *Confession: A Primer*, Holy Theophany Orthodox Church. Retrieved from https://www.theophany.org/orthodox-faith-confession.php, August 2021
22   Malachi 3:3 NKJV

if it was true that he had to sit there in front of the fire the whole time the silver was being refined. The man answered that yes, he not only had to sit there holding the silver, but he had to keep his eyes on the silver the entire time it was in the fire. For if the silver was left even a moment too long in the flames, it would be destroyed.

The woman was silent for a moment. Then she asked the silversmith, "How do you know when the silver is fully refined?" He smiled at her and answered, "Oh, that's the easy part - when I see my image reflected in it."

In discovering a new way of loving God, one will unquestionably be called to endure the flames of trials, temptations and tribulations to prove their loyalty to God. For sure there is a feeling of shame associated with my sin, and no doubt the challenge of exposing myself before God and my priest in confession augments that suffering. However, consider the words of Pope Benedict XVI during his visit to Treviso:

"There can be no love without suffering, because love always implies renouncement of myself, letting myself go and accepting the other in his otherness; it implies a gift of myself and therefore, emerging from myself."[23] Pope Benedict XVI

---

23   Pope Benedict XVI, visit to Treviso, Italy, July 24, 2007. Retrieved from Zenit.org, July 2021

Q5 Why do we need to confess to a priest? Isn't it enough that I have a direct line of communication with God?

It is true that we have been given the gift of open communication with God. The idea that God humbles himself enough to hear and answer each of our prayers is a comforting thought particularly in my journey of repentance. In fact, "openness to God is the precondition for God's dwelling within us."[24] Thus, pouring out my heart before God is a necessary component of offering up genuine repentance. However, there are reasons, three in particular, as to why the church in her wisdom encourages us to kneel before our spiritual elders to partake in confession.

a) The first, and most important, of these three reasons is that the sacrament of confession was instituted by Christ. Christ ordained the priest so that we could receive, through their hands, the saving grace of all of the Sacraments - one of those sacraments being confession. It was directly governed by Christ that the priests of the church would have power to absolve sins in the confines of confession. Following his resurrection from the dead, Christ visited his disciples in the upper room and instructed them saying:

"Receive the Holy Spirit. If you forgive the sins of any, they are forgiven them; if you retain the sins of any, they are retained."[25]

The Apostles continued to emphasise this sacrament by teaching, as exemplified in the Book of James:

"Confess your trespasses to one another, and pray for one

[24] John Chryssavgis, *Soul Mending: The Art of Spiritual Direction*, Holy Cross Orthodox Press, 2000, 22
[25] John 20:22-23 NKJV

another, that you may be healed."[26]

This was the image of repentance and confession in the early church. In actuality, the practise of confession was far more humbling and solemn in the early church than it is today. Whilst today we are required to appear before a priest to attain absolution for our sins; the Christians of the early church were required to confess publicly before the entire congregation in order to receive absolution.

"And many who had believed came confessing and telling their deeds."[27]

b) A second reason to validate the purpose of confessing before a priest is that it humbles us, and this humbling will be a type of vaccination against future temptations. In his book, The Forgotten Medicine, Archimandrite Seraphim Aleksiev writes about confessing in front of a priest saying, "It cures our pride; it makes us blush savingly; it instils in us shame and fear and thus protects us from future sins. When we confess before God, we do so easily, because we do not see him, and it is as if we were talking to ourselves. But what shyness comes over us when we confess before the priest!"[28]

c) Finally, it is so that we may learn to share our burdens with others. The church, as described by St Paul in all its beauty, is the body. As a body, we rely on each member to help carry the weight of our burdens. When the eye wells up with tears, it requires the hand to help wipe them away. This is most true when discussing the burden that sin places on the body as John Chryssavgis says, "we need others because often our wounds are too deep to admit,

---

26   James 5:16 NKJV
27   Acts 19:18 NKJV
28   Seraphim Aleksiev, *The Forgotten Medicine: The Mystery of Repentance*, 35-36

the evil too painful to confront by ourselves."[29] Confession helps us lay our burdens on those who have taken on the responsibility of carrying them.

There is a beautiful story in The Ladder that highlights the power of this practise. There was once an enthusiastic brother in the monastery who was burdened heavily by a particular temptation for many years. For over twenty years he tired himself with fasting and prayer in order to overcome this particular vice, but to no gain. He then purposed to write this temptation on a piece of paper, approached his father of confession, handed him the paper and bowed down before him ashamed of his sin. The elderly monk looked at the piece of paper, smiled and then said to him, "My son, put your hand on my neck." The brother did so. "Very well, brother. Now let this sin be on my neck for as many years as it has been or will be active within you. But from now on, ignore it."[30] From the moment he rose up from the ground, he was never burdened with the temptation again.

Q6
Every time I confess, I am confessing the same sin. How do I shake off the persistent sin so that I can stop embarrassing myself in front of my father of confession?

This is a good question. Perhaps one that most people, if not all people, ask at some point throughout their spiritual struggle. No doubt we all have countless faults, but there is always that one sin that we can pinpoint as our kryptonite. The sin we can't shake off. And so, whenever we approach our father in confession, we'll try word it differently each time or put a new spin on it, so he doesn't recognise that

---
29   John Chryssavgis, *Soul Mending: The Art of Spiritual Direction*, Holy Cross Orthodox Press, 2000, 55
30   John Climacus, *The Ladder of Divine Ascent*, Step 23, 213

it's the same problem we keep coming back to him with.

There is a solution, though no doubt it is one of many. The solution is best explained by a nice little story I once heard about a man praying with his pastor. A man was praying with his pastor at the altar. He prayed a prayer the pastor had heard a few times before. "Lord, take the cobwebs out of my life." Just as he said this, the pastor interrupted and said, "Kill the spider, Lord."

What is the meaning of this story? Many times, we ask God to remove the sin (cobwebs) out of our lives but we don't put the effort in removing the opportunity (spider) to sin.

It reminds me of a formula that was once presented to the youth by Fr Mark Basily from St Mark's Parish in Sydney. He refers to it as the "TOS" formula. The formula looks as such:

Temptation + Opportunity = Sin

What he is proposing is this. While we can't remove the temptations present around us, and sin is inevitable; the one thing we do have the power over is opportunity. For example, if you know that going into your room with your phone may cause you to look at something bad on the internet, then leave your phone outside. If you know that the number one cause of arguments with your mum is not cleaning your room, then wise up and clean your room.

Phillip Snyder recalls a story of his favourite pair of khaki-coloured slacks and an unfortunately placed piece of bubble-gum that put all this in perspective for him. Whilst working in the computer lab of the BYU Harold B. Lee Library teaching his freshman English class, Phillip sat at the front desk and pressed his leg on the underside of the computer table. When he pulled his leg away, he noticed it had attached itself to a freshly planted piece of gum that had firmly implanted itself on his favourite slacks. In a state of panic, Phillip called an end to the class and rushed to his wife who suggested he send the slacks immediately to the dry cleaners and hope they could resolve his issue. Thankfully, upon retrieving his slacks, he noticed that they had been perfectly cleaned and did not appear to have ever been dirtied by the gum. From that point forward, Phillip was particularly careful not to dirty himself whenever he wore these slacks. He would specifically monitor tables and chairs for stray gum before sitting down.

Upon reflecting on his own obsession, he concluded that human beings were a lot like slacks and were prone to being dirtied or stained by "hard to get off" sins; sins that were persistent and stubborn – like gum. He concluded, that to prove our desire to be clean to God, "first, we do our best to reject opportunities to sin. Second, when becoming unclean in moments of ignorance or weakness, we put ourselves in a position that allows us to reinforce our commitment to keep the commandments by humbling ourselves and by following the prescribed steps to complete repentance."[31] Although this only presents one method amongst many others to overcoming your persistent sin, and the power of the Holy Spirit remains the most necessary component, the mindset of removing opportunity puts the individual in the best situation to avoiding the apparent 'embarrassment' of going to their father of confession with the same issue.

However, on this note of embarrassing oneself before their father of confession, it is important to be aware that there is no sin, whether repeated or not, that the priest has not already witnessed. Though some sins may be more difficult to disclose, particularly if I have disclosed them many times before, there should be no shame in constantly pleading for

---

[31] Phillip A. Snyder, *The Bubble Gum Battle: A Perspective on Repentance*, The Church of Jesus Christ of Latter-Day Saints. Retrieved from churchofjesuschrist.org on August 2021.

the forgiveness of my sins before the priest. In The Sayings of the Fathers, the writer recalls a famous tale of a monk who approached Abba Sisoes and enquired, "Father, what should I do? I fell." To which, Abba Sisoes simply replied, "Get up!" The young monk then returned to him and said, "I got up father, and I fell again." Again, Abba Sisoes replied, "Get up again!" A third time, the young monk came to Abba Sisoes and asked, "I have fallen again, for how long should I get up when I fall?" To this Abba Sisoes responded, "Until your death!"[32]

Q7 I confess regularly but I don't feel different after I have had confession

The first thing to say about this is that forgiveness of sins is in no way dependent on feelings. I am forgiven whether I 'feel' different or not. In the same way that I should confess continually whether I 'feel' like it or not. In saying this, there is one feeling that is borne out of continual repentance; that is, "love".

In the story of the sinner woman the Lord tells those who rebuked her:

"Do you see this woman? I entered your house; you gave Me no water for My feet, but she has washed My feet with her tears and wiped them with the hair of her head. You gave Me no kiss, but this woman has not ceased to kiss My feet since the time I came in. You did not anoint My head with oil, but this woman has anointed My feet with fragrant oil. Therefore, I say to you, her sins, which are many, are

---

[32]   Benedicta Ward, *The Sayings of the Desert Fathers*, Cistercian Publications, 219, part 38.

forgiven, for she loved much. But to whom little is forgiven, the same loves little."[33]

With every effort I put in towards turning my heart to God, I draw nearer to the fullness of His unconditional love for me. Metropolitan Anthony Bloom shares a very beautiful personal story in an article he penned on prayer. I would be doing it a disservice by paraphrasing it so here it is in full:

"I remember many years ago my spiritual father asking me, "Do you enjoy praying?" I replied, "Yes." He continued, "Do you pray a lot?" I said, "Yes." "What happens to you," he asked, "if you have had a very hard day and feel so tired that you simply can't pray anymore?" I responded, "I feel very uneasy." "Hmm," he said, "the ceiling may fall on you if it is not supported by your prayers?" So, quite reluctantly, I said, "Yes, yes." And he said, "You know what that means? It means simply that it is not in God's love or concern or providence that you trust; it's in your prayers. You think that you can give him so much praying and he will pay you back with so much care." I did not feel happy about what he said, but I had nothing much to say in response. What he added was even worse. He said, "Well, you must learn to trust God." What a rewarding thought! "And to do that," he said, "I forbid you to pray at all. Before going to bed you will say five times, together with five prostrations to the ground, 'At the prayers of those who love me, save me.' And then you will go to bed, and not one prayer more. But you should then begin to ask yourself, who are the people who love you? Into whose care and under whose wings or protection are you safer than through your own begging? And when a face emerges, a name comes to mind, thank God for them, thank them for their love and rejoice in the fact that you are secure in their love." The first time I went to bed after the exercise, I felt extremely bad. I looked at the ceiling, and then I began to ask myself, "Now, who?

---

33   Luke 7:45-47 NKJV

Who are the people who love me?" It was quite easy in fact: There was my mother, my grandmother, my father, this or that person, and more—my spiritual father, among others! That night, I never reached more than a small circle of people, because I fell sleep. But gradually, as I went day after day remembering those under whose wings I was safe, it even occurred to me that God loves us! The first days I concentrated on people, but then I realized: The Lord Jesus Christ loves me. "Our Father who is in Heaven" loves me. The Mother of God loves me. My guardian angel loves me. The saint whose name I bear loves me. And so, I began to feel safe and, in the process, I discovered something about the communion of saints: I am safe because I am loved. According to what I deserve, I am damned because I am no good. But according to the love that both God and other people give me gratuitously, I can hope—madly perhaps—for salvation."[34]

The more I turn to God in repentance and confession, the more I experience a tremendous love for the One who loved me first. Perhaps, like in the story above, it may not occur overnight and it requires two actions. The first, as is quite clear in the recount, is persistence. In the spiritual life, whether that be in prayer or confession, it is important to persevere in order to gain any sort of benefit. The second action, which is also clear in Metropolitan Anthony Bloom's story, is to be obedient to the instructions of the priest. There is an old Egyptian proverb that reads: "On the son of obedience, rests blessings." This is abundantly clear in the life of Abraham who reaped incredible blessings due to his persistent obedience to the commands of God – despite their challenging nature.

There is a story of two monks who both confessed to the same spiritual father. As this father was located on a

---

[34]   Metropolitan Anthony Bloom, *The Life of Prayer*, Theology Today 61 (2004), 35-36

mountain above the monastery, the two monastics thought it wise to visit him together so they wouldn't have to travel alone. On the way back, the younger monk was rather solemn while the older monk could barely contain his glee. The younger of the two, noticing the stark difference in their moods, enquired of the older monk asking, "why do you feel so happy whenever you confess with him? What does he tell you?" To which he replied, "probably the exact same thing he tells you."

The younger monk, being more aggrieved now, followed up and asked, "so how come you are satisfied when you leave him, and I'm left feeling no different to when I came?"

The older monk smiled and replied, "maybe because I take every word he tells me as though it were from the mouth of God Himself."

Thus, these are two keys to unlocking the true value of confession. The more I persist in confession, the more I will be forgiven. The more I am forgiven, the more I will love and feel loved. The more I feel loved, the more I yearn to overcome my sin. It's no wonder the sinner woman fell at the feet of the Lord.

Q8. Is there a process that I should follow in confession or a particular way to behave? How am I supposed to go about confessing so that I get the most benefit out of it?

There is no right or wrong answer here. There is no formal process of confession other than organising with a priest an appropriate time to meet with him and confess your sins. However, there are some things that we are encouraged to do in order to get the most benefit out of our time in confession. The way I'll break it up is as follows: things to do before, during and after confessing.

a) Before
These days, we often find ourselves waiting outside confession alongside other people who are also waiting for their turn. It can be easy for us to get distracted by this crowd of people, or maybe a friend of ours is also in line with us and we've begun talking with them. This distraction can take away our spirit of repentance. Before confessing with Abouna, spend the time waiting in prayer and spiritual reading. Bring with you a book on repentance (such as this one) and read while you wait. Oftentimes, I have seen people come to confession with their Agpeya (Book of the Hours), reading psalms up until the moment they are called in for their turn. There are also very appropriate prayers in the Agpeya that are suitable to read before confessing such as "the prayer of repentance" and "the prayer before confession." This time should be spent contemplating our sins and our deep need for forgiveness so that we may enter confession with a sincere and repentant heart.

b) During
During confession it is important that we maintain an aura of humility. We are not putting on a show, but by kneeling

at the feet of the priest and by having our heads facing the ground, we are reminding ourselves of our sinful nature and our need for healing. It is important that we recognise how small we are in the face of God who has the power to forgive us our sins and renew us.

c)   After

It is easy for us to leave confession and forget all about it up until the next time we are due to meet with our father of confession. There aren't really many practises in place within the church that we generally follow after we have confessed; besides being encouraged to partake in the Eucharist as early as possible to complete our communion (or reunion) with Christ. Although, I did learn something from a dear friend of mine that changed my approach to leaving confession. I discovered that he would often go to confession carrying a little notepad. The first few times I figured it may have been just a coincidence, but the third time I witnessed it I purposed in my heart to approach him about it and find out his reason why. His response was as follows: "After confession, I sit down with my little notepad and write down what it is my confession father told me I should do. I keep this book handy to keep me accountable to the plans we set in place for my spiritual life so that next time I meet up with him we can review it together."

I found this practise extremely beautiful. It adds a very special seriousness or strictness to the concept of confession and something that we may learn to practise ourselves.

Q9 When should I be repenting/confessing?

The church is built on the concept of 'continual' change. St Paul in his second letter to the Corinthians writes, "Therefore, if anyone is in Christ, he is a new creation; old things have passed away; behold, all things have become new."[35] We are called to always remain in Christ, which means that I need to be near Him always if I wish to remain new. With that in mind, if we think back to our introduction and focus on the quote by Archdeacon John Chryssavgis, we will find the answer to our question of "when":

"Repentance is simply a new way of loving God every day."[36]

If every day I have the opportunity to love God in a new way, in a spirit of renewal, then it logically follows that every day I must live in repentance. It also makes sense given that the nearer I draw to Christ, the more my flaws are revealed to me, thus enhancing the need for repentance. If not for spiritual growth, at the very least to avoid feelings of regret.

Fyodor Doestoevsky, one of the greatest Russian authors of all time, recalls an experience from his late twenties that he refers to as "the turning point in his life." Doestoevsky was brought up as part of the upper class of Russians in the mid 19th century. However, he served to help liberate the working-class slaves that were being oppressed by those deemed 'privileged.' After being captured as part of a large revolutionary group, he was arrested and placed in

---

35   II Corinthians 5:17 NKJV
36   John Chryssavgis, *Soul Mending: The Art of Spiritual Direction*, Holy Cross Orthodox Press, 2000, ix

a maximum-security prison in 1849. The conditions were so terrible that he, along with the other prisoners, were forced to sleep on hard straw beds in small, rain-damaged rooms that had no light. This living arrangement lasted 8 months before the prisoners were taken out of their cells and led to carriages.

They were not warned of their sentence but, given the mildness of their crimes, expected their punishment to be light. As the carriages came to a halt, the prisoners were taken to the gallows and forced to line up. Their sentence – death by gunfire. Without even the chance to gather their thoughts, they were each given a cross to kiss, an opportunity to confess before a priest and then dressed in wretched clothes and prepared for execution. As the first few men were tied up to some stakes, the soldiers took aim and held their positions. Just at that moment, a loud drum roll was heard and a herald riding a horse rode in carrying a pardon for the prisoners from the Tsar.

The prisoners were returned to their cells with the view of sending them to a prison in Siberia. Later, in a letter he wrote to his brother, Doestoevsky explains his new outlook on life following his close encounter with death:

"When I look back on my past and think how much time I wasted on nothing, how much time has been lost in futilities, errors, laziness, incapacity to live; how little I appreciated it, how many times I sinned against my heart and soul – then my heart bleeds. Life is a gift, life is happiness, every minute can be an eternity of happiness."[37]

In a novel he authored later in his life titled, 'The Idiot', Doestoevsky portrays an execution scene akin to the one he faced in his life. He writes about the thoughts of a

---

[37] Fyodor Dostoevsky, *Under the Gun*, St. Petersburg, 1849. Retrieved from laphamsquarterly.org on January 2021

youthful victim awaiting death in a way that makes it clear these were certainly his own personal thoughts from his experience. He says, "What if I didn't have to die? I would turn every minute into an age, nothing would be wasted, every minute would be accounted for."[38]

This is the mentality one should approach their own lives with. Each moment not spent in repentance, in loving God newly, is a moment wasted. It is a moment not worth living. Instead, my life should reflect the life of the church - a life of continual repentance. That is a life of no regrets.

Q10 How can I live a life of unceasing repentance?

If you read the answer to the last question then your next question is likely to have been, "that might be nice in theory, but how am I supposed to turn that into practise?"

The story of St Moses the Black is an extreme example of someone living a life of continual repentance.[39] Following his conversion to Christianity, Moses joined the monastery under the spiritual guidance of Bishop Isidorous. It was this bishop who would become Moses' confession father. One night, bothered by his past sins, Moses woke Isidorous from his sleep thirteen times to confess. Whenever he remembered a past fault of his that had not been addressed, he got up and confessed. Whenever he was burdened by a wicked thought as a residue of his previous life, he got up and confessed. He did not allow a single flaw to be left unaddressed so that he may remain in a repentant state

---

38   Fyodor Dostoevsky, *The Idiot*, Penguin Classics, 2004, Part 1, Chapter V, 108

39   Benedicta Ward, *The Sayings of the Desert Fathers*, Cistercian Publications, 138

and be clean always.

This, as already mentioned, is a very extreme example of living a life of constant repentance. There is a simpler way, however. St Paul, in his letter to the Ephesians, encourages them to "put on the whole armour of God"[40] in order that they may be able to withstand the attacks of the devil. One of the articles that he assigned to them was the "helmet of salvation"[41] ; essentially emboldening them to recall to mind all things pertaining to salvation at all times and in this way remain secure and spotless.

Again, how is this practical? Brother Lawrence, who served as a lay brother in a Carmelite monastery in Paris during the 17th century, offers a solution. The book, 'The Practice of the Presence of God,' is a collection of Brother Lawrence's letters and writings that teach that the easiest way to invite the presence of God into our lives at any moment is to send up small prayers during mundane tasks. For example, while he washes the dishes he would pray: "Lord, as I wash these dishes clean from their filth, also cleanse my heart from all its impurities." On this concept he also elaborates:

"He does not ask much of us, merely a thought of Him from time to time, a little act of adoration, sometimes to ask for His grace, sometimes to offer Him your sufferings, at other times to thank Him for the graces, past and present, He has bestowed on you, in the midst of your troubles to take solace in Him as often as you can. Lift up your heart to Him during your meals and in company; the least little remembrance will always be the most pleasing to Him. One need not cry out very loudly; He is nearer to us than we think."[42]

---

40   Ephesians 6:11 NKJV
41   Ephesians 6:17 NKJV
42   Brother Lawrence. *The Practice of the Presence of God.* New York: Fleming H. Revell Company, 1895

By inviting God into all trivial tasks during the day, we sustain a "salvation" mindset and remain in a state of repentance, struggling against the worldly thoughts that try to plague our minds constantly. One simple prayer to keep handy in our hearts and minds always is the Jesus Prayer – a prayer famously revived in the twentieth century by the release of a popular book titled, 'The Way of a Pilgrim.' The prayer is as follows:

"O Lord Jesus Christ, Son of God, have mercy on me, a sinner."[43]

The idea behind the Jesus Prayer is assumed to be that, by invoking the name of Christ and pleading for mercy in the face of temptation, the power of His name is capable of delivering us. As written in the book of Proverbs:

"The name of the Lord is a strong tower; The righteous run to it and are safe."[44]
So then, the key to living a life of unceasing repentance is simple; it is to live a life of unceasing prayer.

---

43   E. French, *The Way of a Pilgrim and The Pilgrim continues his Way*, Harper, San Francisco, 1991, 7
44   Proverbs 18:10 NKJV

Q11 I'm scared that God won't forgive me again for a sin that I've committed 1000 times.

The question here is essentially, "is it possible that God could ever give up on me?" Because that's what this question is asking by suggesting that there is a limit to God's forgiveness; that He could effectively give up! This is contrary to the promises that we read in the Bible.

In Lamentations chapter 3 we read: "Through the Lord's mercies we are not consumed, Because His compassions fail not. They are new every morning"[45]

It is a direct promise that we have been given regarding the boundless, unending compassion of God. That every morning we awaken to find that His mercy has become renewed. There is no limit to infinite love. We often forget that God is a loving Father who wants nothing more than the very best for His children. And He knows, more than anyone, that the very best for each of us, is that we are established in His home - no matter how long it takes for Him to help us there.

Imagine a son that has run away from home and found himself lost in the woods. The father spends days looking for him until, when he finally finds him, he is found to be dirty, malnourished and cold. In that moment, will the father of this child look at him and say, "how could you leave the house and run away like that? You are never welcome back into my home?" Or would he say, "you look hungry, let's get you something to eat," or, "you look cold, let's get you warm." For sure this would be the response of

---

[45] Lamentations 3:22-23 NKJV – this is read every Good Friday in the 12th hour when God completed our salvation. A reminder that His infinite mercy and love for humanity ultimately led Him to die on the Cross.

a loving father who has found his son.

It's the same with our Father in Heaven. He often finds us broken and bruised, lost in a wilderness of our sins. However, no matter how many times He comes and finds us after we've run away into those woods, His response will always be the same:

"You look hurt, let's get you home."

Q12 How can I make confession of more benefit to me if I often don't feel changed afterwards?

A priest and a soap maker were once walking down the street side by side (not the beginning of a bad joke I promise). The soap maker, looking around, turned to the priest and said, "Your Gospel, the one you spend your life preaching, hasn't done a lot of good for the world has it? Just look around. There is so much evil in the world and a lot of evil people committing that evil. What change has your gospel made?"

The priest remained quiet until the two of them walked by a child who had dirtied himself by playing with mud in a nearby park. Taking advantage of the opportunity, the priest said to the soap maker, "I see that your soap hasn't done a lot of good for the world either; look at how much dirt exists and the world, and so many dirty people too!"

The soap maker said, "Well, soap is only useful to someone when they choose to apply it."

To which the priest responded, "Exactly, so it is with the Gospel."

We forget that confession is a two-way street. Often, we confuse confession for strictly our own personal outlet where we go and confess just to ease our burden of sin, without realising there is an individual who imparts counsel as to how to overcome those sins. If we leave confession without applying the guidance of our spiritual father, no doubt we will never experience any level of benefit and feel changed. Similar to the story of the two monks we explored earlier. One of them benefited and felt the joy of confession because he took every word as though it were from the mouth of God himself. We too ought to approach confession with the same mentality. I am dirty and the priest is offering me soap – it's up to me whether I choose to use it or not.

Q13 How long should my repentance take?

There are two ways to observe this question. The first is, how long should it take for my repentance to garner a reaction from God? And the second is, how long will I be living in a repentant state before I am released from my trials?

From the moment I take that first turn towards Christ, until the end of my days on earth, I will be living in a constant struggle of repentance. That is the nature of the spiritual life. Nevertheless, that does not necessarily mean that God will take a lifetime to respond to one's repentance (if that is how you perceived this question).

In his book, The Return of the Prodigal Son, Henri Nouwen writes:

"From God's perspective, one hidden act of repentance,

one little gesture of selfless love, one moment of true forgiveness is all that is needed to bring God from His throne to run to His returning son and to fill the heavens with sounds of divine joy."[46]

It only takes one act of repentance to invite the response of God. However, it takes a lifetime of struggle to continue to live in that state of repentance.

St Paisios tells the story of a monk who once lived in Karyes on Mount Athos. He was infamously known for being an alcoholic who got drunk on a daily basis and became a scandal to the pilgrims who would venture to Mount Athos. Eventually, he passed away, relieving some of the faithful who approached St Paisios and told him that they were delighted to be rid of the problem of the 'Drunk Monk.'

Father Paisios replied saying, "I knew of the death of this beloved monk, after I saw with my own eyes the legion of angels that came to collect his soul." The pilgrims were astounded, some even protesting the words of the saint suggesting that he may not have understood who it was they were talking about.

To this Father Paisios replied with the story of this saint:

"This particular monk was raised in Asia Minor, shortly preceding the invasion by the Turks when they gathered all the young boys. In order not to take these boys from their parents, they would take them to the reaping. To stop them from crying on these expeditions, they would put a little raki in their milk so that they would sleep."

Raki is a Turkish unsweetened, hard alcoholic drink that is popular in the Balkan region.

---

[46] Henri J.M. Nouwen, *The Return of the Prodigal Son*, Doubleday Publishing, 1992, 116

Father Paisios continued, "Therefore, he grew up as an alcoholic. Then, when he arrived to Karyes, he came across an elder and confessed to him that he was an alcoholic. The elder instructed him to perform prostrations and prayers every night, and to plead with St Mary to help him reduce by one the number of glasses he drank. After a year had passed, he managed with struggle to reduce the number of glasses he drank to 19 glasses from 20. The struggle continued for many years until he finally reached 2-3 glasses, with which he would still get drunk."

The pilgrims listened as Father Paisios' next words put them to shame:
"The world, for many years, saw an alcoholic monk who outraged the pilgrims, but God saw a fighter who fought a lifelong struggle to reduce his passion."
This saint lived a life of daily repentance from the day he turned his life over to God up until the day God sent his army of angels to retrieve him and grant him rest from his struggles.

Q14 What if I find myself rehearsing my confession? Is that wrong?

In the spiritual life, intention is everything! No matter how hard I try, I cannot deceive myself. Meaning, only I will know my true intentions behind every action I take. For example, let us look at the story of Rahab, from the book of Joshua.

Rahab was a harlot living in the city of Jericho when the Israelites sent in spies to explore the city. When guards of the city began looking for them, the two spies hid in Rahab's house. Whilst hiding in there, they made her a promise. The promise was that if Rahab was to help them escape, they would grant her protection when Israel came to invade the land. Rahab agreed and without hesitation, lied to the guards about the whereabouts of the two foreign spies. Now we need to make one thing very clear - under no circumstances is it good to lie, not even this one. In fact, it was not because of her lie that God saved Rahab, but because of her intention. St Augustine reiterates this himself saying:

"Therefore, no lie is just. Accordingly, when examples of lying are proposed to us from the sacred Scriptures, either they are not lies but are thought so for not being understood, or, if they are lies, they are not to be imitated because they cannot be just. As for its being written that God dealt well with the Hebrew midwives and with Rahab the harlot of Jericho, He did not deal well with them because they lied but were merciful to the men of God. And so, it was not their deception that was rewarded, but their benevolence; the benignity of intention."[47]

And so, with this in mind, we come back to our original question - rehearsing confession. If we are rehearsing our confession so that, in some sly way we may win the favour of our father of confession, then our intentions are impure. Sometimes, and it's completely human to think so, we think that if we tell our confessions as they are, then we would make a complete fool of ourselves before the priest (which is kind of the whole point anyway). Because of this, we try to manipulate the story of our sin to make it seem less serious than it really is. This type of rehearsal steals the spirit of repentance away from us.

On the other hand, if we are rehearsing our confession so as to not forget our sins for when we sit before the priest, then our intentions are pure. However, might I suggest another way of not forgetting your sins? Write them down.

---

47   Augustine, *Against Lying*, ACCS on Joshua, 17

This maintains our spirit of repentance before God and the diligence in attending confession with our sins prepared is not overlooked by God.

There is a beautiful story I once heard as a young boy that I have never forgotten to this day. There was once a young girl who was getting ready to attend church one Wednesday night with her mother for a night of confession. So that she would not forget her sins when she sat before the priest, the young girl took a piece of scrap paper and wrote down all the sins she could remember. She held tightly onto this piece of paper as she got into the car and strapped on her seatbelt. On the way, another car ran a red light and collided with the mother and her young daughter. The girl was killed instantly. At the scene of the heart-breaking accident, the girl was found still clutching onto this piece of paper. But when it was taken out of her hands to be read, the paper was blank - her sins had been wiped clean.

God rewards us for our intentions. If they are pure, then He is bound to not forget us. This young girl intended to confess and confess with diligence. Even though she did not arrive at the feet of her father in confession, the Lord accepted her repentance and forgave her sins, because her intentions were righteous.

Q15 Should I be concerned about the repentance of those around me also, or only on my own?

In his first epistle to the Corinthians, St Paul uses the metaphor of a 'body' to describe the characteristics of the church. In the midst of his explanation he proposes the following thought:

"For as the body is one and has many members, but all the members of that one body, being many, are one body, so also is Christ.
And if one member suffers, all the members suffer with it"[48]

This sheds light on the value of caring for the repentance of those around me – for in doing so, I am caring for the body I belong to. Should my eye shed a tear, I would need my hand to wipe it clean. The same goes for the body of the church – should a fellow member suffer; it is my duty to lend a compassionate hand.

It all comes down to the simple fact that we were not created to live alone.[49] When I am alone, I am more prone to attacks from the devil. Dietrich Boenhoeffer writes:

"Sin demands to have a man by himself. It withdraws him from the community. The more isolated a person is, the more destructive will be the power of sin over him, and the more deeply he becomes involved in it, the more disastrous is his isolation. Sin wants to remain unknown. It shuns the light. In the darkness of the unexpressed it poisons the whole being of a person" [50]

48 1 Corinthians 12:12;26 NKJV
49 1 Genesis 2:18 NKJV
50 Dietrich Bonhoeffer, *Life Together: The Classic Exploration of Christian*

It is natural to want to be alone in my sin, in my failings, however, this is where I become most vulnerable. We have been given the gift of community to help strengthen us in times of repentance. In the book of Acts, which recounts the tales of the early church, it is written that the Apostles would return frequently to Jerusalem to spend time in prayer and breaking of bread "in one accord," in order to encourage one another in their ministry. Hence, placing further emphasis on the true worth of community within my own life of spirituality.

Ironically, it is in my repentance, my turning towards God, where I will best learn to appreciate the value of caring for those around me. Dorotheus of Gaza set out to illustrate this in the form of the following image:

"Take a compass and insert the point and draw the outline of a circle. The centre point is the same distance from any point on the circumference... This circle is the world and God is the centre; the straight lines drawn from the circumference to the centre are the lives of human beings. The closer these are to God, the closer they come to each other; and the closer they come to each other and to the world, the closer they are to God." [51]

It is clear then that we must place importance on the repentance of those around us for three reasons:
1.   We are of the same body
2.   Community makes our spirituality stronger
3.   In drawing nearer to others, we draw nearer to God

To put it more poignantly, in the words of St Anthony the Great, "Our life and our death is with our neighbour. If we gain our brother, we have gained God but if we scandalise our brother we have sinned against Christ."

Community, Harperone, 1991, 77
51   Dorotheus of Gaza, *Discourses and Sayings*, pp. 177-179.

Q16 — What if I feel like I don't have a major sin to confess?

The first thing that must be stated regarding this question is this: "If we say that we have no sin, we deceive ourselves, and the truth is not in us."[52] It is a trap from the devil when we convince ourselves that we do not possess a sin great enough that requires confessing, worse still, when we convince ourselves that we are free of any blemishes. Imagine not washing the shirt you wear to work for weeks on end just because it does not have any obvious stains. This ignores the colour it will no doubt lose as well as the worse issue of the stench that it will no doubt develop.

Moreover, this may perhaps be the biggest barrier or obstacle to coming to confession – waiting until you fall into what may be deemed a major sin before seeing a priest. The reason likely being due to the fact that it is the major sins that often weigh us down with heavy burdens that we yearn to be relieved of. What we fail to appreciate is how it is the little sins which, in truth, have the capacity to destroy us more quietly. That is why the brothers of the Shulamite woman in Song of Songs say, "Catch us the foxes, the little foxes that spoil the vines,"[53] knowing that it is the small foxes that enter the vineyard silently that have most potential to ruin it.

On this point, Archimandrite Seraphim Aleksiev writes: "The small sins are often more dangerous than the greatest crimes, because the latter weigh heavily on the conscience and insist on being atoned for, confessed, settled, erased,

---

52 1 John 1:8 NKJV
53 Song of Songs 2:15 NKJV

while the small sins do not weigh much on the soul, but they have that perilous property of making it insensitive to the grace of God and indifferent to salvation. Fewer people have perished from ferocious wild beasts than have from small microbes invisible to the naked eye."[54]

When we learn to acknowledge the little sins as having great consequences on the state of our spiritual lives, we will cease to see them as small, nagging defects and rather, as large, troublesome evils.

The great Saint Macarius was once walking on the street when a carriage pulling a cart of cucumbers drove by. As it drove past him, a cucumber fell off the cart and landed at his feet. Macarius, not thinking twice, picked up the cucumber and ate it. After satisfying his craving, he began to weep over the cucumber as it had not been paid for and this thought weighed heavily on his conscience. It was written that he repented over this stolen cucumber for many years.

Whilst this may seem like an extreme response to an honest mistake (if it can even be called one), it reveals the heart of Macarius, who would not allow even the slightest error corrupt his heart and cause him to deviate from his godly life. St Paul further encourages this strictness in eliminating the little evils that threaten to ruin us:

"But among you there must not even be a hint of sexual immorality, or any kind of impurity, or of greed, because these are improper for God's holy people."[55]

For St Paul, there is no grey area. Sin is black and white. And he recognises that even the slightest hint of sin has the capacity to destroy those who belong to God.

---

54   Archimandrite Seraphim Aleksiev, *The Forgotten Medicine: The Mystery of Repentance*, 32
55   Ephesians 5:3 NIV

Q17 How am I to know if something is a little sin that needs confessing or not?

The spiritual life, as difficult as it may sound, is a journey towards attaining perfection. This means that anything that falls short of that standard, being Christ who was the perfect man, requires closer observation under the microscope of confession.

St James sets the bar as follows, "to him who knows to do good and does not do it, to him it is sin."[56] This assumes that while I may be serving diligently, failure to reach out to a friend, who I know may need a helping hand, falls short of the standard. Whilst I may give my tithes to the church frequently, actively walking past a homeless man without offering even the smallest thing misses the mark. The definition of sin then changes to include not only the evils committed but the good that is left undone. It is a terrifying standard to follow, but it is the Christ-standard. Even our intentions behind doing good will be examined. In 'The Prodigal God,' Timothy Keller writes the following:

"Repentance is not listing your wrongdoings as the older brother "never disobeyed" his Father. That is pharasaical repentance when we only feel remorse or regret over our mistakes. To truly become Christian, we must also repent over the reasons we ever did anything right."[57]

Of course, all of this requires both discernment and awareness. Perhaps there are little sins or deceptively bad intentions in my life that are slowly corroding my

---

56 James 4:17 NKJV
57 Timothy Keller, *The Prodigal God: Recovering the Heart of the Christian Faith*, Dutton, 2008, 77-78

relationship with God that I am unaware of. The solution to this is to come into the light.

What does this mean?

Imagine you are wearing a white shirt. As you look down on it, you find that it is clean, spotless and capable of being worn out of the house. Then you walk into a brightly lit room and, all of a sudden, you look down to find that there are spots of mud and dirt all over the shirt which you could not see before. You could not see them before because you were standing outside of the light. It is the same thing in our relationship with God. Oftentimes there are evils that quietly take us away from God that we cannot see because we are living outside of his presence. Solomon says that, "The way of the wicked is like darkness; they do not know what makes them stumble."[58] He suggests that living in that darkness makes them blissfully unaware of what it is that is leading them astray. Being aware of my sin allows me the opportunity to return to God as it was in the case of the lost son who, after "he came to himself,"[59] found it in his heart to return home to his father. Or, put more eloquently, "sin is the measure of our estrangement from God, but our awareness of sin can be the occasion for our return to him."[60]

Coming into the light and seeing myself for who I truly am, with all my flaws and shortcomings, requires me to come into real communion with God through genuine worship. On this Metropolitan Isaiah of Denver writes:

"The fullness of worship unfolds in sounds, sights, smells, tastes, touch – all your senses. They may not all be engaged in every experience of worship, but they all will be at some time. Whatever the situation of worship, there must be a

---

[58] Proverbs 4:19 NKJV
[59] Luke 15:17 NKJV
[60] John Chryssavgis, *Soul Mending: The Art of Spiritual Direction*, 41

heart in tune with God, or you will simply be going through the motions, and your heart and soul will be still."[61]

When my heart is in tune with God, it hears and understands better the things that please and displease His heart.

Running parallel with this new founded awareness is discernment to distinguish between good and evil. It is a virtue not easily understood but possibly best defined in Thirty Steps to Heaven (an abbreviation of The Ladder) which states:

"Among beginners, discernment is real self-knowledge; among those midway along the road to perfection, it is spiritual capacity to distinguish unfailingly between what is truly good and what in nature is opposed to the good; among the perfect, it is a knowledge resulting from divine illumination, which with its lamp can light up what is dark in others. Discernment is a solid understanding of the will of God in all times, in all places, in all things... an uncorrupted conscience... pure perception."[62]

The beauty about both of these virtues – spiritual awareness and discernment – is that they are found in the same place, on your knees in the purifying presence of God.

However, I will offer one practical tip that was offered to me: ask your father in confession the following – 'is there something you see in me that needs changing that I cannot see myself?'

It never hurts to ask.

---

61 Metropolitan Isaiah, *Turn Around: The Orthodox Purpose Driven Life*, 70
62 Vassilios Papavassiliou, *Thirty Steps to Heaven: The Ladder of Divine Ascent for All Walks of Life*, 197

Q18 — Where can I find motivation to repent and confess when I need it?

In the early 1980's, Scott Hahn was enjoying a life of simple spirituality as a minister in the Presbyterian Church when he began researching the roots of the Passover. As he dove deeper into its origins, he could not help but notice how the life of the early Church focused on the Eucharist and what it commemorated. This led him down a path of transformation as he began to embrace the Catholic church and her liturgy as he "quite literally hungered for the Eucharist."[63] His entire conversion, like the life of the church, like the life of repentance and confession, centred around the understanding of the Eucharist.

If repentance is 'loving God in a new way' and it requires one to undergo a deep spiritual struggle, then it can be logically concluded that the Eucharist, which remembers the moment where love and suffering came together, offers the greatest motivation for returning to God. In this, Scott Hahn spoke truth when he implied, "Love is the answer to the riddle of suffering. Suffering is the answer to the riddle of love. Only with Jesus – and specifically with the Paschal Mystery – did God reveal the answer to the perennial riddles of our existence. Love turned his suffering into an offering at the Last Supper, and that love is the Eucharist."[64]

By partaking of the Eucharist, we share in that Love and the knowledge that sacrifice drives the individual to seek a life consumed by that love no matter the cost. Repentance

---
63   Scott Hahn, *The Fourth Cup: Unveiling the Mystery of the Last Supper and the Cross*, Image, 155
64   Scott Hahn, *The Fourth Cup: Unveiling the Mystery of the Last Supper and the Cross*, Image, 176,180

and confession, though it is a journey of struggle, is made easier in the presence of the Eucharist.

Consider this quote from St Cyril the Patriarch of Alexandria in the 4th and 5th century. Though lengthy, it perfectly summarises the power of the Eucharist to lead to repentance:

"If the position of pride is swelling up in you, turn to the Eucharist; and that Bread, which is your God humbling and disguising Himself, will teach you humility. If the fever of selfish greed rages in you, feed on this Bread; and you will learn generosity. If the cold wind of coveting withers you, hasten to the Bread of Angels; and charity will come to blossom in your heart. If you feel the itch of intemperance, nourish yourself with the Flesh and Blood of Christ, who practiced heroic self-control during His earthly life; and you will become temperate. If you are lazy and sluggish about spiritual things, strengthen yourself with this heavenly Food; and you will grow fervent. Lastly, if you feel scorched by the fever of impurity, go to the banquet of the Angels; and the spotless Flesh of Christ will make you pure and chaste."[65]

The knowledge of Christ's sacrifice alone is sufficient enough to lead one to their knees in repentance. The partaking of it – overwhelming.

---

[65] Cyril of Alexandria, *A homily on Turn to the Eucharist*. Retrieved from allsoulscoventry.org.uk on August 2021

Q19 What if I have been away from the Church for too long? Is there any way back for me?

Maybe you're the type of person who grew up within the walls of the church as a child. Your dad was a deacon, your mum served in Sunday school and your Sundays were dedicated to life in the church. Somewhere along the way, you might have gotten a little bored, or maybe, in your mind, you 'grew out of it.' Eventually, the mundane routine of waking up every Sunday and getting dressed for church became meaningless and so you stopped going. Possibly, this went on for years and you believe that there's no way back for you. You might even feel that if you chose to go back now, no one would look at you the same. You'll always be a "foreigner."

If you feel this way, you're not alone. But you would be wrong. We become foreigners only when we leave the Church. You could never be a foreigner in the home of your Father. Christ says it Himself when He said:

All that the Father gives Me will come to Me, and the one who comes to Me I will by no means cast out.[66]

He says, "the one who comes to Me, I will by no means cast out." He doesn't lay out any conditions for coming to Him either. He doesn't say, "you can come, but wash up first." He doesn't say, "come all you like but make sure you've prayed all the hours of the psalms first." No! He says, "no matter how broken you come, no matter how long you've been gone, come to Me, and you will not be cast out. You will not be treated like a foreigner."

---
66   John 6:37 NKJV

More than that, if the story of the Prodigal Son teaches us anything it's that, even if I've been gone for so long, even if I have made myself estranged from Him, God will go out of His way to find me once more. While reflecting on the story of the Two Lost Sons, Henri Nouwen suggests that even when I am estranged from the Father, He is still so near and prepared for our repentance.

"God is there. God's light is there. God's forgiveness is there. God's boundless love is there. What is so clear is that God is always there, always ready to give and forgive, absolutely independent of our response. God's love does not depend on our repentance or our inner or outer changes. God's only desire is to bring me home."[67]

There is a story of an English clergyman who lived around the 18th century by the name of Robert Robinson. He was a very talented pastor who used to love writing poems and hymns for his congregation. However, after many years, his faith began to dwindle and he essentially, 'grew out of it.' He left his service and moved to France, enjoying the passing pleasures of sin for years. One evening, he found himself on a carriage ride with a famous Parisian socialite who had recently come to find Christ. She was eager to get his opinion regarding some poetry that she had been reading at the time. She read out to him the following words:

"Come thou Fount of every blessing, Tune my heart to sing thy grace. Streams of mercy never failing, Call for hymns of loudest praise."

When she looked up, she found him to be crying bitterly. He caught his breath and looked at her. "What are my thoughts

---

[67] Henri J.M. Nouwen, *The Return of the Prodigal Son*, Doubleday Publishing, 1992, 78

on it?" he gently asked in a croaking voice, "I wrote it. And now I see how I have strayed so far away from Him, that I can never find my way back."

"But don't you see," the woman replied, "the way back is written right here in the third line! 'Streams of mercy never ceasing!' Sir, those streams have been flowing your whole life, even here in Paris tonight."

That very night, Robert turned back to his life with Christ. And he was never a foreigner again.

Q20 If I still suffer the consequences of my repeated sin even after I've repented and confessed, does that mean I am not forgiven?

There is a difference between being forgiven and suffering the consequences of your sins. An example of this in the bible is King David. After committing adultery and murder, King David spent one year unrepentant for his sins. When finally confronted with his error, King David faces up to it and repents bitterly. The prophet Nathan, who made David aware of his sins, responds to his repentant cry and says, "The Lord also has put away your sin; you shall not die. However, because by this deed you have given great occasion to the enemies of the Lord to blaspheme, the child also who is born to you shall surely die."[68] His sin was forgiven, but he still had to suffer the consequences. Similar to a smoker who quits after many years of smoking. Sure, he no longer suffers from the addiction, but the damage he has caused to his body is still there, and he is still prone to many illnesses.

---
68   2 Samuel 12:14 NKJV

Q21 When in confession do I ask about a personal problem like a problem at school or with parents?

The primary purpose of sitting before our father of confession is to uncover our sins and attain forgiveness. However, there is always a temptation to discuss social issues or seek career advice knowing there is wisdom in the words of our spiritual guide. Whilst this is not an inappropriate use of our time in confession, it is important to know that it comes secondary to my actual confession. Once I have exposed myself before my father of confession, then I can discuss more worldly matters with him and seek his guidance.

Q22 I commit the same sin so often that I've lost the feeling of regret for my sin. How can I be more sensitive to this sin?

This is the danger of repeated sin, when I develop a sense of numbness towards it. There are a number of strategies we can utilise to overcome this; however, I will just offer two.

The first is to make the sin you have become numb to the focus of your prayer for a period of time. To request from God that he reveals to you the things that cause you to stumble into this repeated sin and ask him to remove the traps you constantly fall into. Fr Matthew the Poor offers a beautiful prayer entreating this very thing from God saying:

"Show me my defects. Reveal to me my sins. Show me my faults. Make me to understand what I have burdened You with. Make me to understand what trespasses I have committed & which have slipped my mind & heart & now stand as a barrier between You & me. Make me to know Lord, make me to know."[69]

The second thing, and more importantly is, if I become insensitive to sin, I need to become more sensitive towards Christ. In this way I will inherently feel the weight of my sin all the more. The way I accomplish this is again by the way of prayer, and consistency in my prayer is key. At the beginning of the book of Isaiah, the prophet is placed face to face with the throne of God. Following his interaction with the King of kings, Isaiah utters the following words:

"Woe is me, for I am undone! Because I am a man of unclean lips, And I dwell in the midst of a people of unclean lips; For my eyes have seen the King, The Lord of hosts."[70]

This is not dissimilar to Peter, who after witnessing the power of Christ in the miracle of the catching of the fish, fell to his knees and proclaimed:

"Depart from me, for I am a sinful man, O Lord!"[71]

Both Isaiah and Peter recognised the gravity of their sins when they came face to face with God. When they became sensitive to their Master, they innately became sensitive to their errors.

---

[69] Matthew the Poor, *A Starting Prayer*, Accessed on YouTube
[70] Isaiah 6:5 NKJV
[71] Luke 5:8 NKJV

Q23 Is there benefit to remembering my sins?

The concern with continual remembrance of our sin, as we have previously mentioned, is developing a feeling of despair that threatens to keep us separated from God. However, there are circumstances in our lives where the remembrance of our sins can be to our benefit.

The first is during times when we are receiving praise from others. By remembering my former sins, I remind myself that I am unworthy of any praise and the praise is due to Christ who delivered me from my past life. I remind myself that I am no better than the person whose praise I am receiving. I remind myself that any goodness they see in me, belongs not to me but to the Lord like David proclaims.[72]

Another benefit to remembering my sins can be found in my service towards others. How can I share in the sufferings of others, if I cannot first acknowledge the suffering within me caused by battling my sins. Fr Matthew the poor says,

"A servant will not be able to sympathize with the weak and outcast if he does not first live with the constant awareness of his own weakness, his own inadequacy."[73]

Furthermore, the remembrance of my sins can often be a good tool to help draw me back into the presence of God. It is my way of saying to God, "look Lord how you delivered me, look where I am now because of your love for me. And still I have much to grow in my journey towards you." The

---

72 Psalm 16:2 NKJV
73 Matthew the Poor, *If You Love Me: Serving Christ and the Church in Spirit and Truth*, Ancient Faith Publishing, Chesterton, Indiana, 1980, p25

midnight praises are beautiful in that, they are the only prayers in the church where we don't make any requests before God. Rather, we simply praise him and acknowledge our sins; we elevate him and lower ourselves. This is done by the remembrance of his deliverance as we recurrently reference the Exodus from Egypt, the wars won against the enemies of Israel and the kings defeated at times when hope seemed lost. In remembering the weakness of the Israelites during those moments and the power of God in the liberation, we intrinsically remember our own times of weakness and how God delivered us also.

Conclusion

The little boy rushed around the house, making sure everything was in order for when his father came home. He dusted the cabinets, washed all the dishes and swept the floors before heading back to the kitchen to make sure all the utensils were placed away. His mother watched curiously as he then began setting the table and cleaning the living room that he had made messy the day prior. He ran back to his room and ensured his bed was made and he had picked up all his things from the floor in case his father happened to walk in and admonish him for being disorganised. He then returned to his mother and asked her if there were any further chores that needed completing. She replied by expressing her gratitude for all his efforts and reassured him that his father would be very pleased with the state of the house. Then, with a small grin on her face, she looked into her little boys' eyes and asked him, "why did you leave this all to the last minute, it could have been cleaned earlier this morning?"

To which the little boy replied, "I'm sorry mum, I should

have cleaned it all this morning, but I slept in."

In his epistle to the Ephesians, St Paul instructs the church the way in which they should walk now that they have become imitators of Christ. After teaching them that they ought to walk in the light of Christ he then proclaims:

"Awake, you who sleep, Arise from the dead, And Christ will give you light." [74]

We have already said that repentance is many things. It is a journey, it is a shared experience, it is a constant struggle and, of course, it is a new way of loving Christ on a daily basis. However, we cannot come to the conclusion of a book on repentance appropriately without mentioning one more thing we know it to be – an awakening.

St Theophan the Recluse, in his book 'Turning the Heart to God,' writes of this concept that "the awakening of a sinner is such an action of God's grace in his heart that he, having awakened from his sleep, sees his sinfulness and feels his danger." [75]

It is the moment when an individual begins to look inwards and become aware of their own sinful nature. It is a moment shared by the Prodigal Son who "came to himself" before rising from the filth of his sin and returning to his father's home.

This book holds no value without this message. All the verses, quotes and stories in the world could not inspire one to journey back to the Father's home, they are simply an alarm for one to recognise it is time to wake up. The responsibility then falls on the individual to ensure they do

---
74   Eph 5:14 NKJV
75   Theophan the Recluse, *Turning the Heart to God*, Concilar Press, 13

Conclusion

not continue to press 'snooze.'

I will leave you then with the words of St Paul who reiterated his message to the Church of Rome. A call to repentance. A call to take ownership of your salvation. A call to wake up.

"Now it is high time to awake out of sleep; for now, our salvation is nearer than when we first believed. The night is far spent, the day is at hand. Therefore, let us cast off the works of darkness, and let us put on the armour of light. Let us walk properly, as in the day, not in revelry and drunkenness, not in lewdness and lust, not in strife and envy. But put on the Lord Jesus Christ, and make no provision for the flesh, to fulfill its lusts."[76]

---

76   Romans 13:11-14 NKJV

Final Words

"Are you a sinner? Do not become discouraged, and come to Church to put forward repentance. Have you sinned? Then tell God, 'I have sinned.' What manner of toil is this, what prescribed course of life, what affliction? What manner of difficulty is it to make one statement, 'I have sinned'? Perhaps if you do not call yourself a sinner, you do not have the devil as an accuser? Anticipate this and snatch the honour away from him, because it is his purpose to accuse. Therefore, why do you not prevent him, and why do you not tell your sin and wipe it out, since you know that you have such an accuser who cannot remain silent? Have you sinned? Come to Church. Tell God, 'I have sinned.' I do not demand anything else of you than this. Holy Scripture states, 'Be the first one to tell of your transgressions, so you may be justified.' Admit the sin to annul it. This requires neither labour nor a circuit of words, nor monetary expenditure, nor anything else whatsoever such as these. Say one word, think carefully about the sin and say, 'I have sinned.'"
- St. John Chrysostom (On Repentance and Almsgiving, Homily 2)

Section 2

For She Loved Much

Introduction

"And behold, a woman in the city, who was a sinner..." (Lk 7:37)

Of all the ways one's story could be introduced; this is how the woman in chapter 7 of Luke's Gospel was presented to the audience. Furthermore, from generation to generation, this woman would be recognised as the 'sinner woman,' it has become a part of her biblical identity. And yet, of all the examples of repentance littered throughout scripture, hers is perhaps the most profound.

In the eyes of the Lord, she was not the 'sinner woman' or the 'adulterous one,' she was the woman who "loved much." So, who was she? What did her life look like prior to her encounter with Christ?

Undoubtedly, if you are familiar with the tale, you have more than likely construed an image of this woman's life prior to her presentation in Luke chapter 7. A life filled with lust, greed, pleasures, lewdness and general immorality.

Still, there remains a question surrounding the challenges she faced. How did people greet her in the street? How did she carry herself within the public eye?

St Ephraim the Syrian offers a beautiful contemplation on what the sinner woman's path may have looked like directly preceding her coming face to face with the Lord. His homily "For She Loved Much" is a poetic retelling of her story, one that should continue to be told for generations to come.

Our book began with a story of repentance where the feet of one was washed by another. It is only fitting then that we conclude with the feet of Christ himself being washed by the tears of one who represents all repentant sinners. As you read through this poignant tale and join the sinner woman in coming nearer to the feet of Christ, may you reflect on the words prayed directly before partaking of the Eucharist:

"As You did not stop the adulteress from kissing Your feet, please do not prevent me from coming near You to receive Your Holy Body and Your sacred blood."

For She Loved Much

The Gospel According to St Luke

(Luke 7:36-50)

A Sinful Woman Forgiven

Then one of the Pharisees asked Him to eat with him. And He went to the Pharisee's house, and sat down to eat. And behold, a woman in the city who was a sinner, when she knew that Jesus sat at the table in the Pharisee's house, brought an alabaster flask of fragrant oil, and stood at His feet behind Him weeping; and she began to wash His feet with her tears, and wiped them with the hair of her head; and she kissed His feet and anointed them with the fragrant oil. Now when the Pharisee who had invited Him saw this, he spoke to himself, saying, "This Man, if He were a prophet, would know who and what manner of woman this is who is touching Him, for she is a sinner."

And Jesus answered and said to him, "Simon, I have something to say to you." So he said, "Teacher, say it."

"There was a certain creditor who had two debtors. One owed five hundred denarii, and the other fifty. And when they had nothing with which to repay, he freely forgave them both. Tell Me, therefore, which of them will love him more?" Simon answered and said, "I suppose the one whom he forgave more." And He said to him, "You have rightly judged." Then He turned to the woman and said to Simon, "Do you see this woman? I entered your house; you gave Me no water for My feet, but she has washed My feet with her tears and wiped them with the hair of her head. You gave Me no kiss, but this woman has not ceased to kiss

My feet since the time I came in. You did not anoint My head with oil, but this woman has anointed My feet with fragrant oil. Therefore I say to you, her sins, which are many, are forgiven, for she loved much. But to whom little is forgiven, the same loves little." Then He said to her, "Your sins are forgiven." And those who sat at the table with Him began to say to themselves, "Who is this who even forgives sins?" Then He said to the woman, "Your faith has saved you. Go in peace."

For She Loved Much
By: Saint Ephraim the Syrian

Beloved, read and find comfort in God's mercy. He forgave the offenses of the sinful woman. He upheld her when she was afflicted. The Lord opened the eyes of the blind with clay, that he might see light. He granted healing to the paralyzed man, who arose, walked, and carried his bed. He gave us the pearls - His Holy Body and Blood. He brought His medicine secretly and with them He heals openly. He wandered around the land of Judea, like a physician, bearing His medicine.

The Woman's Decision

Simon invited Him to the feast, to eat bread in his house. The sinful woman rejoiced when she heard that He sat and was feasting in Simon's house. Her thoughts gathered together like the sea, and like the large waves of the sea, her love surged. She beheld the Sea of Grace, how it had forced itself into one place. She resolved to go and drown all her wickedness in its large waves.

Because of her sins, her heart was bound with chains and tears of suffering. She began weeping and saying within herself, "Of what help is this fornication? Of what benefit is this lewdness? I defiled innocent ones without shame. I corrupted the orphan. Without fear, I robbed merchants of their merchandise. My greed was not satisfied. I have been like a weapon used in war, killing both good and bad. I have been like a storm on the sea, sinking many ships. Oh, how I wish I could have met and won just one man who could have corrected my lewdness! But, few are of God. Many are of Satan."

She began to change her outward appearance. She washed away her eyeshadow, which blinded her. Tears gushed forth from her eyes over her seductive makeup. She took off and cast away the enticing bracelets and jewelry of her youth. She took off and cast away her clothing of fine linen and the garment of prostitution. She resolved to go and clothe herself in the garment of repentance and reconciliation. She took off and cast away her decorated sandals. She directed her steps on the heavenly path.

She took up her gold in the palm of her hand and held it up to the face of heaven. She began to cry secretly to the One who hears openly, "This, O Lord, I have gained from my sins. With it, I will purchase salvation. This I gathered from orphans. With it I will win over the Lord of orphans."

The Woman Buys the Ointment

She took her gold and an alabaster flask and went forth quickly while weeping. She went to the perfumer. The perfumer saw her and wondered. He began questioning the harlot, "Wasn't it enough for you to corrupt our whole town? What is the meaning behind your clothing today? You took off your promiscuity and clothed yourself in modesty. Up until now, whenever you came to me, your appearance was different. You were dressed in fine linen and brought little gold. Before, you only asked for precious ointment for seduction. But now! Why are you dressed like this? Either clothe yourself according to your behavior or buy ointment according to your clothing! The ointment you are buying now is not suitable to what you are wearing.

"Have you met a merchant who can bring you great wealth? Doesn't this merchant prefer your lewdness? Is this why you are now clothed so modestly? Oh, but if he truly is a chaste man who loves modesty, then woe to him! Into what has he fallen? He has fallen into a gulf that will swallow up his merchandise. Take the advice of someone who desires your well-being. Send away your many lovers, who have never helped you since your youth. Seek one husband who can make you pure."

The sinful woman answered, "Do not stop me, sir. Do not stop me with your questioning. I asked you for ointment, not freely, but I will pay you its value willingly. Take my gold, as much as you ask for, and give me the precious ointment. Take that which endures not - my gold - and give me that which does. I will go to Him Who endures, and purchase that which endures.

"What you have said about a merchant - yes, a man has met me today Who bears riches in abundance. He has robbed me and I have robbed Him. He stole away my transgressions and sins. I have robbed Him of His wealth. What you have said about a husband - yes, I have won to myself a Husband in heaven, Whose dominion stands forever, and of His kingdom there will be no end."

Satan Tries to Stop Her

The woman took the ointment and went quickly. Satan saw her. At one moment, he rejoiced, but in another moment, he was enraged and grieved greatly. He rejoiced because she carried perfumed oil. But then he saw her dressed so modestly, and he was afraid. He clung to her and followed her closely, just as a thief follows a merchant. He listened to her murmur softly. He closely watched her eyes to see where her glances were directed. He moved close to her feet in order to mark her direction.

Satan is very crafty. He learns our aim from our words. Therefore, the Lord taught us not to raise our voice when we pray, that the Devil may not hear our words, draw near, and become our adversary.

When Satan saw that he could not change her mind, he disguised himself as a man, and stood in a crowd of young men, like her previous lovers.

Satan said, "Tell me, where you are going? Why are you in a hurry? You seem to hurry more than usual. What is the meaning behind your meekness? Your soul is as humble as a maidservant's. Instead of garments of fine linen, you wear filthy weeds. Instead of bracelets of gold and silver, you do not even wear rings on your fingers. Instead of decorated sandals, you are not even wearing worn shoes. Reveal to me the reason for your actions, because I do not understand the change that has come over you. Has one of your lovers died? Are you rushing to bury him? We will go with you to the funeral and share in your sorrow."

The sinful woman answered, "Yes, you have rightly said that I go to bury the dead. My sins have died and I go to bury them."

Satan replied, "I tell you, O woman, that I am the first among your lovers. I will give you more gold than before."

The woman said, "I am tired of you and you are no longer my lover! I have won a Husband in heaven, Who is God. His dominion stands forever and of His kingdom there will be no end. I will say it again. I have been a slave of Satan from my childhood until this day. I was a bridge and he walked all over me. I destroyed thousands of men. My eye-makeup blinded my eyes. I was blind among the many whom I blinded. I became blind and was ignorant of the One Who gives light to the blind.

"But now! I go to receive Light for my eyes, and by that Light to give light to many. I was bound and did not know that there is One Who overthrows idols. Behold! I go to have my idols destroyed so that I may destroy the recklessness of many. I was wounded and did not know that there is One who heals and binds up wounds. Behold, I go to have my wounds bound."

Satan's Plan

When Satan heard her wise words, he groaned and wept. He cried out, "I am conquered by you, O woman! I do not know what I shall do!"

At His Feet In Confession

Once again, Satan realized that he could not change her mind. He began weeping for himself and said, "My source of pride has perished, the pride of all my days. How can I lay a trap for this woman who ascends on high? How can I shoot arrows at this woman, whose wall is unshaken? I will go into Jesus' presence, since she is about to go there. I will say to Him, 'This woman is a harlot.' Maybe He will reject her and not receive her. Then I will say to Him, 'This woman who comes into Your presence is a prostitute. She has led men captive through her prostitution. She has been polluted since her youth. You, O Lord, are righteous. Everyone flocks to see You. If people see You speaking with a harlot, they will run away from You and no one will greet You.'"

Satan said these things at first, but then began to wonder, "How will I enter into Jesus' presence? There are no secrets with Him. Everything is known and revealed to Him. He knows me. He knows who I am. If even by chance He rebukes me, I am undone. All my tricks will be wasted. Since I cannot go to Jesus, I will go to Simon. I will put these thoughts in his heart. I will say to him, 'Simon, tell me about this Man in your house. Is He really a righteous man or a friend of the wicked?'"

Simon heard the words of the evil one and replied, "From the day I first saw Him, I have not seen any lewdness in Him. Rather, I see quietness, peace, and humility. He heals the sick without expecting any reward in return. He cures diseases freely. He stands by the grave, calls out, and the dead rise.[77] Jairus asked Him to raise his daughter to life, trusting that He could. As He went on the way, He healed a woman, who touched the hem of His garment. Her bitter pain left her at once.[78]

---

77 John 11:1-44
78 Mark 5:21-43, Luke 8:40-56

"He went into the wilderness and had compassion on the hungry. He made them sit down on the grass and fed them out of His mercy. [79] In the boat, He willfully slept, and the sea arose against the disciples. He rose and rebuked the wave and wind, and there was a great calm.[80]

"The widow, left alone, followed her only son to the grave. He consoled her, gave him to her, and gladdened her heart.[81] By His voice, He healed the blind and mute man.[82] He cleansed the lepers by His word.[83] He restored strength to the limbs of the paralyzed.[84] He opened the eyes of the blind man, who was afflicted and weary, and he saw the light.[85] For two others who sought Him, He opened their eyes.[86]

"As for me, I have heard about the fame of the Man, and I invited Him to bless my possessions, and to bless my flocks and herds."

Satan answered Simon, "Do not praise a man at his beginning, until you learn his end. Until now this Man has been sober and does not take pleasure in wine. If, by the time He leaves your house, He does not speak with a harlot, then He is a righteous man."

Satan said these things cunningly to Simon. Satan then stood back and watched what happened next.

79	Matthew 14:13-21, Mark 6:30-44, Luke 9:10-17, John 6:1-14
80	Matthew 8:23-27, Mark 4:35-41, Luke 8:22-25
81	Luke 7:11-17
82	Matthew 12:22-30
83	Luke 17:11-19
84	Mark 2:1-12, John 5:1-15
85	John 9:1-41
86	Matthew 20:29-34

At Simon's House

The sinful woman, full of her transgressions, came standing by the door of Simon's house. She clasped her arms in prayer and wept at the door saying, "Blessed Son, Who descended to the earth for the sake of man's salvation, do not close Your door in my face. You have called me and, behold, I come. I know that You have not rejected me. Open for me the door of Your mercy, that I may enter, O Lord, and find refuge from the evil one and his hosts! I was a sparrow and the hawk pursued me. I fled and took refuge in Your nest. I was a heifer and the yoke burdened me. I will return to You. Lay upon me Your yoke, that I may take it on me, and work with Your oxen."

Simon, the master of the house, looked and saw the woman. The color of his face changed and he addressed her saying, "Get out of here, harlot, for the Man who visits this house is a righteous man. His friends and companions are blameless. Wasn't it enough for you to corrupt our whole town? You corrupted the chaste without shame. You robbed orphans and did not so much as blush. You plundered the goods of merchants without shame."

The woman answered Simon and said, "If there is anyone at your feast who wishes me to come in, He will call for me."

Simon closed the door and stood afar off. He lingered a long time and did not tell anyone at the feast about the woman at the door. However, He, Who knows what is hidden and secret, signaled to Simon and said, "Come here, Simon. Is anyone at the door? Whoever it is, open for him and let him come in. Let him receive what he needs and then go. If he is hungry, behold, in Your house is the Bread of Life. If he is thirsty, behold, the Blessed Fountain is in your dwelling. If he is sick and asks for healing, behold, the Great Physician is here. Allow sinners to behold Me. For their sakes, I humbled Myself. I will not ascend to heaven, to the place from which I came down, until I bring back the sheep that wandered away from the Father's house. I will lift the sheep on My shoulders and carry it to heaven."

Simon answered and said, "My Lord, this woman who stands in the doorway is a harlot. She is lewd and polluted from her childhood. You, My Lord, are a righteous man and everyone is eager to see You. If men see You talking with a harlot, they will leave You and no longer greet You."

Jesus replied, "Whoever it is, open, and let her come in, and you will not bear any of the blame for this. Though her sins are many, I ask you to receive her without rebuke."

Simon returned to the door, opened it, and told the woman, "Come in and do as you will."

The sinful woman, full of transgressions, came forward and stood by His feet. She clasped her arms in prayer and said, "My eyes have become like streams that do not stop watering the fields. Today, they wash the feet of Him Who seeks after sinners. This hair, abundant since my childhood - do not prevent it from wiping this holy body. This mouth that has kissed the lewd, do not forbid it from kissing the body that forgives transgressions and sins."

Simon stood afar off to see what He would do to her. He Who knows the secrets of the heart signaled to Simon and said to him, "Simon, I will tell you your thoughts concerning the harlot. In your heart you said, 'I called this Man righteous, but the harlot kisses Him. I invited Him to bless my possessions, but the harlot embraces Him.' Simon, there was a certain creditor who had two debtors. One owed five hundred denarii, and the other fifty. And when they had nothing with which to repay, he freely forgave them both. Which of them ought to thank Him more? The one who was forgiven five hundred or he who was forgiven fifty."

Simon answered and said, "He who was forgiven five hundred ought to give greater thanks."

Jesus said to him, "Actually, you are he who owes five hundred, and this woman owes fifty. Simon, I came into your house and you did not bring water for My feet. This woman, whom you called a harlot, who was defiled since her childhood, washed My feet with her tears. She wiped them with her hair. Should I send her away without receiving forgiveness? Most assuredly I say to you, I will write of her in the Gospel."

Then He looked to the woman and said, "Go. Your sins are forgiven and all your transgression covered."

May our Lord account us worthy to hear Him say, "Come, enter, you blessed of My Father, inherit the kingdom made ready for all who will do My will and observe My commandments."

Glory to Him! May His mercy rest upon us at all times! Amen! Amen!

Recommended Readings

1. The Forgotten Medicine by Archimandrite Seraphim Aleksiev
2. Confession: A Series of lectures on the Mystery of Repentance by Metropolitan Anthony (Khrapovitsky)
3. Turning the Heart to God by St Theophan the Recluse
4. The Life of Repentance and Purity by HH Pope Shenouda III
5. Soul Mending: The Art of Spiritual Direction by Archdeacon John Chryssavgis
6. The Imitation of Christ by Thomas é Kempis
7. The Ladder of Divine Ascent by John Climacus
8. Turn Around: The Orthodox Purpose Driven Life by Metropolitan Isaiah of Denver
9. Thirty Steps to Heaven by Vassilios Papavassiliou
10. The Return of The Prodigal Son by Henri J.M. Nouwen
11. The Prodigal God by Timothy Keller
12. Harlots of the Desert: A Study of Repentance in Early Monastic Sources by Benedicta Ward SLG
13. The Sayings of the Desert Fathers by Benedicta Ward SLG

www.ingramcontent.com/pod-product-compliance
Lightning Source LLC
LaVergne TN
LVHW091316080426
835510LV00007B/516